Take Matters Into Your Own Hands: Dream Now!

How to Take Hold of the Life You've Always Dreamed About

Manuel V. Scott

GLIMPSE PUBLISHING
BUFFALO GROVE, IL

Design by Candace Creative Inc.
Library of Congress Cataloging-in-Publication Data

Scott, Manuel V.
    Take Matters Into Your Own Hands: Dream
Now!: How to Take Hold of the Life You've
Always Dreamed About/ Manuel Scott – 1st ed.

ISBN: 1440444048
    1. Self-help. 2. Personal Growth. 3. Success.

CASE: 1-135108003

ISBN: 1440444048
EAN-13: 9781440444043

I DEDICATE THIS BOOK TO

Martin Stokes, for bringing to me a message of life…

Erin Gruwell, for parting the curtains and letting the sun shine in.

My Mom, Bonnie Cooper- my hero.

My sons, Manuel Walter and Christopher Barack, for being my sons.

My soul-mate, Alice-- more dear to me than my own heart's blood.

TABLE OF CONTENTS

INTRODUCTION

By picking up this book, you are beginning something that could truly change the quality of your life forever. I am speaking from experience. For the last ten years, I have had the privilege of traveling around the world, speaking to people from all walks of life. During my travels, I have enjoyed the distinct honor of sitting at the feet of some of the world's most successful people. I have learned that all of them have taken the road "less traveled." They were not born wealthy, and did not inherit any money from rich relatives. Rather, they have made choices, developed habits, adopted certain behaviors that have separated them from the vast majority of people, and have made them very wealthy. They are millionaires, own their own planes, live in very luxurious mansions, and are living their dreams. During my time with them, I asked a lot of questions, and spent time trying to learn their habits, attitudes, and seeking to discover the "secret sauce" of their success.

Much of what they have shared with me is in this book. I am absolutely committed in this book to make sure that you are crystal clear about how to achieve your wildest dreams. All that's required of you is two things. Number one, the desire on your part to learn, and number two, your commitment to read this book, and do the little assignments that I give you to think and work through, as simple or as challenging as the activities may seem at the moment. If you will do that, the things that you used to call dreams will become a part of your daily reality.

Again, I am speaking from experience. I am speaking from the experience of seeing how others have used the tools in this book to improve their own lives. More importantly, I am speaking from the experience of applying the things in this book to improve my own life.

When people see my designer suits, cashmere overcoats, Brooks Brothers shirts, and my silk, Windsor-knotted neckties, they probably could not tell that as a boy I used to wear raggedy, hand-me-down clothes from the Goodwill and Salvation Army; and, that instead of going back-to-school shopping, I had to cut off my jeans' legs, turning them into shorts so they could last another year.

When people see my hand-made, well-shined shoes, they could not tell that I used to put cardboard in my shoes to keep my socks from falling out of the large holes I had in the soles of my Payless shoes; or, that the Nike "swoosh" sign on my shoes was drawn with a black magic marker (when I got to school that day, my classmates quickly pointed out that the swoosh had been painted on backwards!).

When people hear me recite Shakespeare or Kipling, employ iambic pentameter, and discuss existentialism, they would never know that my English grammar was so poor that I was once classified as an ESL student (English as a Second Language).

After seeing my properties, most people couldn't tell that I have been homeless, slept in cars, on beaches, and on the floors of homeless shelters; and, that I lived in twenty-six places by the time I was sixteen years old.

When people see my undergraduate and graduate degrees from U.C. Berkeley and Trinity International University, they would be surprised to learn that I missed about sixty to ninety days of school every year; that during the first semester of my freshman year I earned a 0.6 GPA on a 4.0 scale; or, that I dropped out of high school at the age of fourteen.

Most people would not know, after sharing meal with me at a fine restaurant, that I used to jump into the dumpsters of McDonalds and Taco Bell to find food to eat.

As hard as it is for me to share those memories with you, they are all true.

How did I make such a drastic turnaround? How did I go from being an "F" student to an "A" student; from being a high school drop-out to having a master's degree (and perhaps a PhD in the near future); from being an English as a Second

Language (ESL) student to one who knows Greek and Hebrew- from being "un-teachable" to unstoppable?

More importantly, how can you go from living beneath your potential to realizing your dreams; from being an "F" student to an "A" student; from being broke to being financially free; from mediocrity to excellence; from living check-to-check to enjoying financial freedom?

The answers are in this book.

The fact is, even if you did not go to college, don't have a trust fund, and don't know a thing about Plato, Aristotle, or Socrates, you can achieve your dreams. If you did not do that well in school, cannot read that well, aren't that good at math, you can achieve your dreams. If you don't have any political clout, aren't part of the "in" crowd, or did not get voted the "most likely to succeed," you can achieve your dreams.

Even if you've lived, or are living, in a crack house, a jail-cell, the hardest street corner, the darkest alley, or under the coldest bridge, you can achieve your dreams. History is filled with people who achieved tremendous success in the face of incredible challenges. For example, Chris Gardner whose story is told in Will Smith's "Pursuit of Happyness," Jim Carrey the comedian, Oprah Winfrey the media mogul, and many others are proof that you can rise from poverty to extreme wealth.

How did they do it? They took matters into their own hands. By reading this book, you are going to learn what you need to do in order to take matters into you're your own hands, and transform your reality into the life you've always dreamed about.

The first thing you need to know is this: *Success is a choice.* It is a choice to position yourself to achieve your dreams. You don't just wake up and find yourself successful. In order to qualify for it, you have to make a choice, and the question you have to ask yourself is, "what kinds of things must I choose to do, and what kinds of things must I choose not to do, so that I can position myself to achieve my dreams?"

Robert Frost, the poet, answered that question for us when he penned the following words:

Two roads diverged in a wood, and I—
I took the one less traveled by,
And that has made all the difference.[1]

Walking through the woods on a winding road, under the spreading sunrise, the poet, Robert Frost, came to a fork in the road. He slowed down to think about which of the two roads he should take. One of the roads had on it smashed shrubbery, flattened clumps of grass, and a trampled carpet of wildflowers, because many people had traveled down that road.

I imagine that the other road was robustly green, and had on it clinging gardens, shrubs and low vegetation. The road was dotted with rocks, enclosed with hills. That road was uncultivated

---

[1] Frost, Robert. <u>Mountain Interval</u>. New York: Henry Holt and Company, 1920; Bartleby.com, 1999.

and un-peopled. Compared with the first road, few people had gone down that second road. As such, the second road was the road "less traveled."

Rather than taking the well-worn, grass-trampled road, Robert Frost chose, in his own life, to walk down the road "less traveled." He concludes the poem by saying that his choice to take the less-traveled road had made all the difference in his life.

In the same way, you and I are presented with two roads every day. We can choose the road that most people walk on, or we can choose a path that very few people take. The first road is filled with people who are following the crowd, and who accept mediocrity, being average, and fitting in. It is a road that is filled with people who are choosing to settle for "good enough."

However, the second road- the road with all the shrubs and vegetation- is a road that leads to greatness. It is the road to success, the road to self-realization, the road to living your dreams. The second road has very little traffic. If you take the second road, you will be lonely at times, because you may have to separate yourself from people who do not believe in you.

The road to living your dreams is the "road less traveled," because few people actually make the decision to walk down that road. The road less traveled requires you to leave your comfort zone, and do some things to position yourself for success.

Success begins with the desire for more in life, and making a choice to achieve that desire. I'll say it again: success is not something that just happens to you; it is a choice you must make. How can you make that choice, and specifically, what do you have to do to rise to the realization of your dream?

That's what this book is all about.

As you begin this journey of taking the less-traveled road to achieving your dreams, I want to tell you that I have incredible respect for you, and that I care about you. Even though I may not know you personally, I hope that my caring will come through in the words on these pages. The reason I respect you is because I feel that you and I have kindred spirits. You opened this book, you made an investment, and you are now being proactive about improving the quality of your life. You are ten times further than ninety percent of the people that you and I will meet on the street or in school. Most people who want to improve the quality of their lives have no clue about what it is they want out of life, and worse, they are not willing to do anything to change it. You're at least searching, and for you to be reading this book says to me that you're willing to do what it takes to be successful, and to take matters into your own hands.

Congratulation on beginning this journey upon the "road less traveled."

CHAPTER 1:

WHERE THERE IS NO VISION

She was a young lady who was born blind, deaf, and mute; she could not speak, she could not hear, and she could not see. However, with a fierce tenacity, an unwavering determination, and unrelenting vigor, Helen Keller learned how to read, write, and communicate very well. After thinking about her own condition, and the obstacles she had overcome, she said that *"Worse than being blind is to see but have no vision."*

Too many people can see but they have no vision. Too many people are just coasting through life, from pillar to post, going here and there, without any clear direction. This kind of directionless wandering is merely a symptom of not having vision or a dream.

Vision, more than anything else, affects the attitudes you have, the actions you take, and the decisions you make. Every day, vision determines how you spend your time, who you spend it with, and what you spend it on.

In this chapter, you will learn what vision is, why it is so important for you to have a vision or a dream, and how you can discover your vision or dream, so that you can translate those dreams or visions into reality.

WHAT IS VISION?

Vision is a mental picture about your near or immediate future. Let me break that down for you. Your *reality* is where you are right now. Your reality is the set of circumstances, state-of-affairs, or conditions that you are living with *right now*. However, your *vision* is the set of circumstances, state-of-affairs, or conditions that you see yourself having in your near or immediate *future*. Vision- a clear mental picture of your near or immediate future- gives you the ability to see beyond your present realities, and to become what you not yet are.

For example, your reality may be that you are living in a cramped apartment, fighting over one bathroom, and arguing over who gets the remote control. Your vision, however, may be that you see yourself living in a spacious home that you own, with several bathrooms, and flat-screen televisions in every room. Your reality may be that you are in a line of work where you are not fulfilled, your supervisor is unfair, your pay is low, and your responsibilities are overwhelming; but your vision may be that you will own your own business, you will be the boss, and you will love what you do. Your reality may be that you are shy, soft-spoken, and hate public speaking; but your vision may be that you will be a confident, well-spoken, eloquent person. Your reality may be that you are single, saving yourself for marriage, and refusing to settle for just anybody; but your vision is that you will be in a fulfilling, covenant relationship, with someone who is willing to give to you just as much as you are willing to give to him or her.

Your reality is the current set of circumstances, states-of-affairs, or actual conditions that you are facing right now; your vision is what you will be, the circumstances you will have, the income that you will have, the lifestyle that you will live, the kind of person that you will be.

So let me pause here and ask you, what is your vision, what mental picture do you have in your head about your immediate or distant future? What do you see in your future that takes you beyond your present reality, your current state of affairs, your current conditions, what picture do you see about where you are going, what you are going to become, what you are going to possess, what you are going to enjoy, what you are going to share, what you are going to distribute, what you are going to do? What is your vision? What is your dream? What is your hope? What inspires you, what wakes you up in the morning? What gives you an energy boost when you think about it? What would you do for free because you love it? If you could not fail, what would you do with your life? What is your vision? Where are you going to travel, where are you going to study, where are you going to open that business, where are you going to shop, who are you going to help, what problems are you going to solve, what societal need are you going to meet? What is your vision? What is your dream?

Stop right now, and write down your vision for your life. Write down your dream. Take five to ten minutes to write down where you see yourself being, or what you see yourself doing in the next three to five years. Exactly how much money do you want to make? What exactly are you willing to do to make your dream a reality? When do you plan to achieve this dream (the date)?

VISION GIVES YOU HOPE

If you don't have a vision, then you are stuck in your reality. You have settled with your current situation; you have settled for your current-state-of affairs, you have become complacent with the conditions of your life.

And if you get stuck in your reality, then you are going to be depressed. When you dwell on your reality, you are likely to take up drinking, drugs, violence, or some other coping mechanism. When you are stuck in your reality, then you have nothing to motivate you.

You just go to your job and do the bare minimum; you go to school because everyone says you have to; you give up on your marriage, because you don't see where it's going; you give up on yourself. Without a vision for your life, you settle for second best; you accept mediocrity; you get comfortable with things as usual; you start saying things like "life has no purpose."

But when you get a vision for your life, you get a glimpse of *what can be. You get a glimpse of your own possibilities.* Vision, as such, gives you a mental picture about your future, which then gives you hope. By giving you hope, vision motivates you, encourages you, and propels you forward. Sometimes, vision is all you have to keep you going in the midst of your reality. Vision is the only thing that keeps you getting up in the morning after crying all night; vision is what lets you see yourself as you *will be* even though you are not yet that person right now. Vision gives you hope.

VISION GIVES YOU DIRECTION

Why is vision so important? Stephen Covey says in his book, First Things First, that "[v]ision can become a motivating force so powerful it becomes the DNA of your life. It's so ingrained and integrated into every aspect of your being that it becomes the compelling impetus behind every decision we make. It's the fire within- the explosion of inner synergy that happens…It's the energy that makes life an adventure- the deep burning 'yes!' that empowers us to say "no"- peacefully and confidently- to the less important things in our lives".[2]

When you have a vision for life, you get a sense of direction. It gives you clarity about where you are going, and how you are going to get there, and what it's going to take for you to get there. When you have a vision, you can say no to the less important things so that you can focus on things that will get you closer to your dreams.

Without a vision, your life will be scattered. I read a Hebrew proverb, which says, "Where there is no vision, people get out of hand."[3] The phrase "get out of hand," in the Hebrew language often refers to hair that is hanging loose without a turban, or in modern terms, a "head-wrap" or a "wave-cap."

---

[2] Stephen Covey, A. Roger Merrill, Rebecca R. Merrill, First Things First: To Live, to Love, to Learn, to Leave a Legacy. New York: Simon and Schuster, 1994. P. 105.
[3] Proverbs 29:18, Holy Bible. Author's translation.

Have you ever seen how a woman's hair looks when she has gone to bed without wrapping or rolling her hair the night before? Regardless of her attempt the next morning to style it, it goes in all kinds of directions, doing whatever it wants to do. It looks like it needs conditioner, a retouch, and a miracle.

What I am trying to say is that your life without vision is like hair without a head-wrap- it is all over the place. It's messy, it's not cute; it ain't pretty; it's out of control; and, it's in need of a miracle. Without vision, your life is all over the place.

On the contrary, by inference, life *with* vision is like hair that has had a head-wrap the night before. It is controlled, it is contained, it is trained, and it is going in the same direction. Life with vision is like hair with a wave cap. The hair is wavy, going in the same direction.

The first semester of my freshman year in high school, I earned an "F" in Jazz, a "C" in English, a

"D" in World History, a "D" in Physical Education, a "D" in Band, an "F" in Spanish, and an "F" in Math. I think that averages out to a 0.6 Grade Point Average! If one were to predict what kind of future I would have based on these grades, I have no doubt that the forecast would be grim. My grades were terrible.

The Second semester grades were even better- I dropped out of high school!

I went back to school that following year, and my first semester back, I earned an "A" in Math, an "A" in Drivers Ed., a "B" in English, an "A" in Physical Education, an "A" in Career Guidance, a "B" in Graphic Arts, and an "A" in Life Science.

What happened? How did I go from being an "F" student, to an "A" student? How did I go from being un-teachable to unstoppable?

I was given a vision for my life.

After I dropped out of high school, a man named Martin helped me turn my life around. He helped me see beyond my present circumstances, and get a glimpse of a brighter future for myself. That vision, that dream, that glimpse, inspired me to change.

What was my vision? It was a vision of me breaking the cycle of poverty and pain in my family. It was a vision of me graduating from high school. It was a vision of me creating a better life for my mother and family. It was the vision of me one day owning a home, and being the kind of father that I never had. It was a vision of me empowering others, and giving people hope. That vision literally awakened me from my slumber, and inspired me to make a change.

VISION REQUIRES FAITH

If you don't have a vision or dream, then you have no hope. In other words, you are not hoping for anything if you don't have a dream or a vision of a better future for yourself. If you are not hoping for anything, then you don't need to have faith.

Let me explain the connection between your reality, vision, hope, and faith. What is faith? Faith is the substance of things hoped for. That means that you believe in something so much that you can almost touch, smell it, feel, or taste it. Having faith is being able to "experience" something in your mind before you actually "experience" it with your hands. To have faith means you see something with your "spiritual" eye that is currently invisible to the "natural" eye. Faith is what you need to turn your mental vision into its physical equivalent.

Reality is where you are right now; and, as I have already said, vision is where you see yourself being in the future. Hope is the longing you have in your heart to have that which you see in your future through your vision or dream. And, faith tells you that it is only a matter of time before your vision becomes your reality.

Faith is the substance of things hoped for. In other words, vision is the picture; faith is the substance. Faith let's you almost touch, smell, or taste the picture you have in your head and heart. Faith gives you the substance in your head and heart before you ever touch it with your hands.

Enough of all that mumbo-jumbo. How does all of this work in real life? When I was still a young man in high school, when I was still learning the basics of English grammar- long before I became a public speaker- I saw visions of myself standing before large groups of people, inspiring them with words that I was speaking. Sometimes, when I heard other speakers make presentations during assemblies, I often saw myself delivering my own message in their place.

The same thing happened to me in college, at the University of California at Berkeley. Because of these visions of myself speaking to large crowds of people, I often mentally transformed my little bedroom into a coliseum where an old upright speaker became my lectern, and all the objects in my room became my audience. For hours I would recite poetry and speeches in my empty room.

During college, I worked for peanuts as a "Loss Prevention Specialist"- that's just a fancy name for security guard. It was my job to secure the buildings by making sure all the doors were locked, the lights were off, and the place was empty. Many nights, after all the buildings were secure, I went to the largest ballroom in the building (Pauley Ballroom), and for hours, I recited speeches to an empty room. Eventually, I found myself doing that in the largest venues on campus (such as Wheeler Auditorium), which sat over seven hundred people. I even found a way to practice a few times on the platform of the eighty-five-hundred-seat Hearst Greek Theater. Even though each venue was empty, in my mind, I was speaking to a standing room only crowd of people who were being inspired by my words. I would speak as though the room were packed to capacity with people who needed to hear what I had to say. I would speak, inspiring thousands, painting for them a vision of a brighter tomorrow. I would speak, telling people that in spite of where they come from, they can achieve their dreams. I would speak, and I would see lives being changed.

Mentally, emotionally, and behaviorally I was committed to making that dream a reality.

Not long after that, people began to invite me to be the Master of Ceremony for campus events. I became the guy who was on the microphone engaging, entertaining, and empowering audiences, young and old. Shortly after that, I began receiving invitations at speak to elementary and middle school students. Then I began receiving invitations to speak to high school students. Before long, I began receiving invitations to speak to community organizations. Eventually, I began receiving invitations to speak in other states. Finally, I began to receive invitations to speak in other countries.

Every now and then, when I get a little tired of traveling, I look through testimonials of people who have heard me speak. Here are just a few of the things I read: "Manuel saved a ton of people today." "I've never been so inspired!" "I'm going to stop trying to commit suicide now." "You blessed us with a reminder about what is at stake in the work we do- transformation!" "Few speakers have been able to have that kind of impact." "Everyone needs to hear his message...He's a life changer!" "What a magical night! Manuel has a gift for touching the human spirit." "I came to work this morning with a new perspective." "I never heard a crowd that size be quiet for so long- everybody was just so engaged!" When I read things like this, I am given another boost to keep on going.

I absolutely love what I do. When nobody else believed in me, I had a dream that inspired me. I had a vision for my life that caused me to fall in love with books, and to learn how to summon the English language and send it into battle. In a small room, with a speaker box, all I had was a dream of inspiring people with my words. That small room turned into an empty ballroom. That empty ballroom turned into filled classrooms. Classrooms turned into filled ballrooms, and ballrooms have turned into filled convention centers. A little while ago, I had the privilege of speaking in Hong Kong, China to a Coliseum of twelve thousand people who had traveled from one hundred and ninety-two countries. And, in just a couple of months, I will be speaking to a crowd of 100,000 people!!!

The young man who seemed to have every disadvantage, who was classified as an ESL student; who had a 0.6 G.P.A.; and, who was a high school dropout, now has the privilege of speaking to thousands. Whether I'm in Houston or Hong Kong, Kansas City or Cairo, Los Angeles or London, I love carrying the torchlight of hope into the recesses of dormant potential, and showing the gems that are sparkling there.

It all began with a dream, a vision, for my life.

WHAT IS YOUR DREAM OR VISION?

If you want to achieve your dreams, you need to first figure out what your dreams are. You need to "detect" or "discover" them by asking yourself, "where do I want to end up in life?" So I ask you again, what is your dream or vision?

The following questions are designed to help you discover what your future could look like. You definitely need to take time to write out your answers in your own private notebook or journal, because writing just does something to your mind and heart. It commits you to having something more than wishful thinking. Writing things down tells your mind and heart that you are serious about something. So get to writing, that you can catch a glimpse of your own possibilities!

What are you personally passionate about? If money were not an issue, what would you do for free? Do you love to travel, sing, write, read, teach, preach, dance, or build? Do you like to debate, research, or do experiments? Do you like to play the piano, style hair, design clothes, or handle money? Do you like working on cars, business, or furniture? Think about it, and write down whatever comes to your mind.

Or, what gets on your last nerve? What burdens you? Does disorganization, ineffective programs, inhospitality, irrelevant preaching, or bad music upset you? Your answer to these questions might give you a clue as to what your vision, dream, or calling in life might be. For example, if you get bothered whenever you hear a band playing music poorly, then you might be wired to be involved in music of some sort. If you absolutely abhor it when things are disorganized, you might be wired to be a project manager or planner of some sort. If your heart is pierced with grief and compassion whenever you see homeless people, then you might be a social justice advocate or something like that.

Also, what abilities do you have that others have complimented or affirmed? What can you do better than others? What sets you apart? What unique skills do you have that you can use with very little effort? Are you naturally good at using computers, making music, typing, or negotiation?

Also, what is your temperament or personality-type? Have you taken the DISC, Meyers-Briggs, or some other personality analysis? Are you a dominant person, an influencer, a supporter, or a compliant person? In other words, do you care more about getting things done than you do about people's feelings? Or do you care more about how people feel than you do about getting things done? Are you a behind the scenes person who just wants to help where there is a need? Or, are you a person who is very detail-oriented, and needs to plan for every little thing before you make a decision? You should really take one of these assessments if you haven't already done so, because they help you understand yourself, and they help you see how you tend to relate to others. Such personality assessments also help you understand how to improve the way in which you communicate with others.

Finally, what experience do you have that might help you get a glimpse of your future? What experiences have you had personally, what jobs have you had, what challenges have you faced or conquered which shaped who you are. For example, many women who have been abused would probably be able to counsel and assist others who have been abused. Also, people who have been homeless have a unique way of understanding and relating to homeless people. As such, they might have a vision, dream, or calling to find housing for the homeless.

These are just some questions to help you think about the big picture of your life. Remember, all things have two creations: first things are created in our minds, and then they are created in reality. Therefore, take matters into your own hands, and begin figuring out what your dream, vision, or calling is.

CHAPTER 2:

ROADMAP TO SUCCESS

I was once driving my family from Denver, Colorado to Sterling, a small, rural town in the northwest corner of the state. It was my first time driving to Sterling. Because I had ridden to Sterling as a passenger many times before the trip, I didn't really think the drive would be all that hard to get to Sterling. We had been on the road for about an hour when everyone else in the car had fallen asleep. Since I am an adventurous person, I found myself appreciating the beauty of the scenery and the tranquility of the ride. After a while, I was running low on gas, so I pulled over, filled up the gas tank, and went inside the mini-mart to grab some snacks. While paying for my items at the counter, I let the cashier know I was driving from Denver, and asked him how much longer I had to drive before I got to Sterling. Looking at me in disbelief, he blurted out, "Sir, you're in Nebraska!"

I thought I could make it from Denver to Sterling on my gut feelings, so I never bothered to get a map, and didn't stop and ask for directions. As a result, I ended up in a place that I had no desire to be.

If you want to take matters into your own hands, and turn your dreams into reality, you need to know that having a dream is not enough. You need a "roadmap"- a plan- to get you from where you are to where you want to be, so that you can maximize the use of your time, energy and resources.

Most people have a dream; few people have a map to get there. In fact, most people never take their dreams out of their minds and hearts, and break it down into practical, realistic, written goals. That's called a plan, and that's what you need. Your plan is your map that will get you to your desired destination.

Your plan, or "roadmap" lets you know where to turn left, when to turn right, and how long you are supposed to stay on that road, and when you are supposed to exit.

How do you develop a plan? That's what this chapter is all about.

DETERMINE WHERE YOU ARE

If you want to drive from your house to Disneyworld in Florida, you would need a map to get you from your current address to 3111 World Dr., Lake Buena Vista, FL. Disney World represents your dream; your home represents your current situation, your reality. To achieve your dreams, you drive from your home (your current reality) to Florida (your dream).

Before you get on the freeway, you need to make sure you have enough gas in the car, enough snacks to eat, money and credit cards, enough clothes for the journey, some books or reading materials, some DVDs, an Ipod, and anything else you might want or need. Before you jump in the car and head for Florida, you need to make sure you have what you need for the journey.

In the same way, when it comes to your dreams, before you just begin rushing to make your dream a reality, you want to take an honest, careful, clear-headed look at yourself to make sure you have what you need for the journey. For example, if you want to become a lawyer, but you are still in middle or high school, then the first thing you need to do is look at your grades. How are your grades? More specifically, how well do you read and write? Can you write an essay that has a clear thesis, a body that flows, has supporting arguments, illustrations, transitions, and conclusions?

Also, do you have a hard time making it to appointments on time? Where are you mentally, emotionally, academically, professionally, and physically? How is your credit? How much debt do you have? What are your insecurities? What are your strengths? How is your relationship with your father and mother? Were you abused as a child, or are there any mental or emotional scars that you have for which you need to see a counselor? Are you on academic probation, or are you on the honor roll? Are you a member of any pre-law clubs, or do you know anyone who is a lawyer or judge?

When you own a business that sells products like books, shirts, pants, or video games, you have to take inventory. Taking inventory is required for tax and business purposes, and it lets you know exactly how many goods do you have in your building at any given moment. You go through each of the items in your storage room, and you look carefully at what you have, and then you figure out what you need in order to make sure you have enough items in stock for your customers.

In the same way, if you want to be successful, you have to go into the storage room of your own heart and mind and take inventory. You have to look up and down the aisles, and check how much passion you have in your reserve. How much character do you have? Are you a responsible person? Are you really committed to making it to your destination?

"FORGET" YOUR PAST

Some time ago, my wife, Alice, and I ran in a 10k race. And while I was running in that race, I remember running one mile, and felt a little winded. I made it to the second-mile mark, and I was even more tired. When I made it past the third, and then to the fourth mile, I was literally struggling to keep my legs moving. And something began to happen. I began to think about all of the people I had passed up, all of the miles I had already run, and I began to feel good about myself. I thought about the fact that I had made it 4 miles, a feat that most people could not face. Even though I had about 2 more miles to go, I began to lose motivation. Why? The more I began to think about what I had already accomplished, the less motivated I became to keep moving forward.

In your own race to your dreams, are there any things in your past that are causing you to become complacent? Is there anything in your past that is causing you to be stagnant? Are there any accomplishments, mistakes, awards, or accolades that are limiting your potential? Do you come from a pretty good family? Did you attend some of the finest schools? Maybe you live in an exclusive neighborhood, or live in a very nice house. May I submit to you that you need to stop letting those things of your past negatively influence your present? Why? Because the more you find gratification and satisfaction in your past accomplishments, the less motivated you will be to press forward to newer, and dare I say, greater things.

That's what the word "forget" means. After listing out several of his own accomplishments, one of my role models once said, "This one thing I do, forgetting what lies behind." To "forget" does not mean that we are to force ourselves to have some kind of amnesia or senility about things in our past. While there are some people who seem to have the gift of selective memory, that's not what it really means to "forget." To "forget" means to refuse to let things that happened to you in the past prevent you from living abundantly in the present.

Also, to "forget" is not just a one-time deal. Rather, it is something that you have to keep doing over and over again, because there are several things that happened to you in your past, good and bad, that keep being replayed in your brain, stifling your possibilities, and keeping you from being better than you were yesterday.

What do you need to keep "forgetting" about in your own past? What memory, experience, triumph, or tragedy do you need to release? Your history was merely preparation for something greater. Don't live in it, learn from it, and move on.

WRITE OUT YOUR ROADMAP TO SUCCESS

After you have dreamed, gotten clear-headed about your current situation, and forgotten about some of your failures and accomplishments, you need to write down your plan in your journal. Keep in mind that your plans will probably change as you go, but it is better to have a written plan than to have no plan at all. At least with the written plan, you can learn about what worked and didn't work, and try something else. Without a plan, you are just shooting from the hip without any forethought or deliberation.

What should you write down in your plan? I'm going to walk you through the process below.

I have listed some of my own dreams below:

I dream of myself traveling speaking to people around the world, inspiring and equipping others to overcome their obstacles and achieve their dreams.
I dream of myself being a faithful, loyal husband to my wife.
I dream of being a loving father to my children.
I dream of being healthy in every area of my life: mentally, emotionally, spiritually, physically, and financially.

WRITE DOWN YOUR OWN DREAMS

If money were not an issue, what would you do for free? What do you enjoy doing most? What brings you the most joy? Your answer to these questions might be a clue to help you discover what your dreams are. Whatever your dreams are, list them in the space below. It's okay if you only have one or two. I have included more space for you, just in case you have more dreams.

I dream of myself
I dream of myself
I dream of myself

Now that you have written down a few of your dreams for your life, you need to put together your roadmap for each one of your dreams. In other words, you need a plan to get you from where you are right now to where you want to be? Your roadmap requires that you *set goals, set objectives and determine action steps.* Think of your plan like a staircase. At the top of your stairs is your dream or vision. Think of each individual stair as a goal that you must achieve in order to get one step closer to your dream. How many goals will it take to get to your dream? Or, put another way, how many things do you have to accomplish in order to reach your dream?

SET GOALS

Just pick one of your dreams for now; you can do this again for your other dreams. But for now, just focus on your biggest dream. How many steps do you need to take in order to make that dream or vision a reality? A goal is a step that brings you closer to your dreams. Your goals should be SMART: Specific, Measurable, Attainable, Realistic, and Timely. It is important for your goals to be specific and measurable so that you can be clear about whether you have reached them; you need your goals to be attainable and realistic, which means that it is actually possible for you to achieve them, and you don't set yourself up for failure or extreme disappointment; and, you want you dreams to be timely, meaning they need to have a date next to them so that you can have a deadline to shoot for. If you dream of being a doctor, then your goals would include some of the things listed on the following table:

Dream/Vision: I dream of myself being a doctor who saves lives.		
ORDER OF PRIORITY	**GOAL**	**DEADLINE:** DATE WHEN YOU PLAN TO REACH THIS GOAL
	Graduate from college	
	Work at the best hospital in the world	
	Start my own medical practice	
	Graduate from High School	
	Graduate from Medical School	
	Complete my residency requirements	

Now think of one of your dreams/visions, and then figure out how many goals/steps you will need to take to make it to that dream. List out your own goals in the "**GOAL**" column on the next page.

Dream/Vision: I dream of myself (write your dream here)_____		
ORDER OF PRIORITY	**GOAL**	**DEADLINE:** DATE WHEN YOU PLAN TO REACH THIS GOAL

In my example above, you will notice that my goals are out of order. If I wanted to be a doctor, I would first have to graduate from high school before I could graduate from college. So I would put a number "1" next to "graduate from high school." Then, my next goal would be to graduate from college. So, I would put a number "2" next to "graduate from college." Look at my example below.

Dream/Vision: I dream of myself being a doctor who saves lives.		
Order of Priority	Goal	
2.	Graduate from college	
5.	Work at the best hospital in the world	
6.	Start my own medical practice	
1.	Graduate from High School	
3.	Graduate from Medical School	
4.	Complete my residency requirements	

Now you do the same thing with your own goals. Place them in order. Which one must you reach first, second, third, and so on, in order to achieve your dream? Now go back to your list of GOALS, and prioritize your own goals in the column marked "ORDER of PRIORITY." Do that now.

Great! Now that you have listed out your goals, and now that you have placed them in order of priority, you must now put a date next to each of your goals. If I wanted to be a doctor, I would go to my goal marked with the number 1, and I would need to figure out how long it will take for me to reach that goal. Write that in the column marked "DEADLINE: DATE WHEN YOU PLAN TO REACH THIS GOAL" See my example:

Dream/Vision: I dream of myself being a doctor who saves lives.		
Priority	**Goal**	**DEADLINE:** DATE WHEN YOU PLAN TO REACH THIS GOAL
1.	Graduate from High School	**Summer 2009**
2.	Graduate from college	**Summer 2013**
3.	Graduate from Medical School	**Summer 2017**
4.	Complete my residency requirements	**Summer 2020**
5.	Work at the best hospital in the world	**August 2020**
6.	Start my own practice	**January 1, 2025**

Now go back to your list of GOALS, and figure out the deadlines for each of your own goals. Find a calendar online, and set your own deadlines. If you are not sure exactly when you plan to have reached your goal, try to take a realistic guess at when you plan to reach that goal. Be sure that you give yourself enough time to complete each goal. Be realistic with yourself. Do that now.

SET YOUR OBJECTIVES

Great job! You have written your dream/s down on paper. You have written the goals you need to achieve in order to get you from where you are now to your dreams. You have also listed out deadlines of when you plan to reach your goals. Now it's time for you to get even more specific.

What specific things will you have to do to reach your first goal? If I wanted to become a doctor, my first goal would be to "Graduate from High School." In order to graduate from high school there are certain classes that I have to take. Those are objectives. See my example:

Goal: Graduate from High School
Objective: I need to successfully complete 4 units of English (You could really list each class as *one separate objective*, since each one requires you to complete different assignments. For example Grammar, composition, literature, and poetry are different English classes that you could take)
Objective: I need to successfully complete 3 units of Mathematics (Algebra I, Algebra II, Geometry…)
Objective: I need to successfully complete 3 units of Laboratory Science (Biology, Chemistry, Physics)
Objective: I need to successfully complete 3 units of History and Citizenship Skills (US History, Oklahoma History, US Government, Geography, Econ…)
Objective: I need to successfully complete 2 units of the Same Foreign Language: (Spanish, French, German)
Objective: I need to successfully complete 1 unit of Fine arts: (Drama, music, art…)ɔ

You may have noticed that every goal must have some objectives. Just like goals move you one step closer to your dreams, objectives move you one step closer to reaching your goals.

Now you try. Write your top goal in the space below marked "GOAL." What objectives must you achieve in order to reach your first gosal? Write your objectives in the below spaces. Also, when (due date) do you plan on achieving each objective? Write that date in the "DEADLINE" column.

GOAL:	
OBJECTIVE:	**DEADLINE:** DATE WHEN YOU PLAN TO REACH THIS OBJECTIVE.

DETERMINE YOUR ACTION STEPS

You are almost done! Now that you have your dreams, goals, and objectives, there is just one more step in the planning phases that you must complete. You must now come up with some action steps for

54

each objective. Just like goals get you closer to your dreams, and like objectives get you closer to your goals, *action steps* get you closer to fulfilling your objectives. What is an action step? <u>An action step is exactly what you must do in order to reach your objective.</u> This is the most specific part of your planning process.

Let me show you how it works. If I want to be a doctor, then I would first need to graduate from high school. In order to graduate from high school, I would need to accomplish my objectives (or pass all my classes). One of my objectives is to successfully complete 4 units (or classes) of English (technically, that's four different objectives; one for each class/unit). How do I do that? That's where the action step comes in. The action step tells me exactly what I must do to complete each English class. Let's take a look at my example on the next page:

GOAL: Graduate from High School	
OBJECTIVE: Successfully complete 11th grade English.	
ACTION STRATEGY:	DEADLINE: DATE WHEN YOU PLAN TO DO THIS.
Visit guidance counselor to request the English class that I want	9/1/09
Attend class on the first day of school to get my syllabus from my English teacher.	9/15/09
Check-out books on the syllabus from the library.	9/15/09
List all my assignments and put deadlines next to them.	9/16/09
Read "Freedom Writers Diary"	10/1/09
Write rough draft of reflection paper on Freedom Writers Diary	10/3/09
Edit rough draft of reflection paper.	10/7/09
Write final draft of reflection paper.	10/15/09
Turn in Final draft of reflection paper on Freedom Writers Diary	10/17/09

Notice that every one of your goals has more than one objective. The same thing can be said about objectives, because every objective will have several action steps. It's not that complicated. Just

56

remember, *"Dreams need goals, goals need objectives, and objectives need action steps."*

It's your turn now. List out your top goal in the GOAL box. Then write your top objective in the OBJECTIVE box. Next, write down your ACTION STRATEGIES. If you are not sure exactly when your assignments are due, try to guess at the deadlines for now:

GOAL:	
OBJECTIVE:	
ACTION STRATEGY:	DEADLINE: DATE WHEN YOU PLAN TO DO THIS SPECIFIC ACTION STEP?

Congratulations! You finished your Roadmap to success for one of your dreams. What you just did for one of your dreams and goals, you can now do for every one of your dreams and goals. Start with your dream/vision, and then write your roadmap to get you from where you are to where you want to be (Goals, Objectives, and Action Steps). Take your next goal, and do the same thing for that goal. Just repeat the process for every goal, and you will be one step closer to turning your dreams into reality.

MEDITATE ON YOUR PLAN

Now that you have your plan, your ROADMAP written down on paper, it is important that you let it become your internal GPS system, your internal guide that let's you know when to turn left or right. A GPS system tells you how much farther you have to drive before you need to turn. It beeps when you are getting close to your turn or destination. And if you miss a turn, it tells you what you need to do in order to get back on track.

That GPS system needs to be internalized by you. It needs to dominate your mind. When you wake up in the morning, one of the first things you need to do is look at your plan.

For example, when I was a little boy, we used to live in Colorado. Every now and then, my brothers and I used to visit farms to see the animals. I often would go hang out by the cows. And sometimes I would watch the cows eat. I noticed that cows seemed like they were always chewing. They just look at you, chew, and "moo" while chewing. I learned that cattle make jaw movements (or chew) about 40-60,000 times per day! That's because when they eat, they chew the grass or hay, they swallow it, and because they are ruminants, which means they have a digestive system that allows them to regurgitate their food, they regurgitate their meals, and chew on it some more (that's really gross, by the way!). They turn the cud over in their mouths and then swallow it; they then eat some more, turn it over in their mouths, swallow it, regurgitate it, turn it over in their mouths, and they swallow it again (I call that "doing way too much!"). That's where the phrase, "chewing one's cud" comes from, and it means, figuratively, to meditate or ponder. It means to chew on something in your mind and heart, turning it over again and again.

When it comes to your ROADMAP to YOUR DREAMS, you need to eat, chew, swallow, regurgitate, turn over, and swallow your dream and plan over again and again. In other words, you need to internalize that plan, keep it on your mind, and discuss it with others whom you can trust. That plan needs to be on your mind, in your heart, and on your agenda every day. When you wake up in the morning, your next major goal needs to be on your mind.

I know this sounds like a lot of information. It is. Success isn't going to come easy. Everyone has a dream, but only a few people have a plan. You have just been given tools to write down your plan, and create your ROADMAP to achieve your dreams.

Trust me, I am telling you what I know, and have experienced for myself. When I was a young man, I didn't have a plan. I missed over ninety days of school per year, and earned bad grades. I never did my homework. I never took school seriously. Eventually, I dropped out of school.

However, when I got a vision for my life, and began to see a brighter future for myself, *everything* about my attitude changed. Shortly after returning to school, I set a goal to graduate from high school; I graduated from high school. I had a goal to one day go to college; I graduated from college. I set a goal to go to earn a master's degree; I graduated with a master's degree. I set a goal to buy a home; I now own more than one home. I set a goal to travel the world; I have traveled to four continents. I set a goal to become a professor; I am preparing to begin my PhD program. I don't write any of that to impress you; I write it to impress upon you that I planned my work, and I worked my plan. The fact is, most people don't plan to fail; they fail to plan. If you are serious about achieving your dreams, then you need a plan.

At the beginning of this chapter, I told you about my experience of driving into Nebraska even though I was trying to get to Sterling, Colorado. I got lost because I didn't have a map, and I didn't stop to ask for directions. Eventually, I made it to my desired destination, because I found a map, and asked for directions.

I wrote this chapter to help you draw out your map to success, and to encourage you to stop, determine where you are right now, and figure out what must change in order for you to begin moving in the direction of making your dreams part of you're daily reality. Remember, knowledge is not power; the right application of that knowledge is power. Don't just read this and do nothing. Turn off the television, turn off the music, go to a quiet place, and write out your plan today. Your destiny is there for the taking; it's just waiting for you to show up!

CHAPTER 3:

THE ART OF EXCELLENCE

A man bought a new house, and he noticed that there were a few cracks on the walls. So he bought some paint, and painted over the cracks. A few days later, he noticed some more cracks on the walls, and painted over the cracks again. A few days later, he was walking through his living room, and he saw even more cracks on the walls.

He became frustrated, and called an inspector to help him with the problem. The inspector walked around the house, and came back to the owner of the house and said, "sir, you don't have any problems with your walls." And the owner, irritated by the inspector's assessment, responded, "Yes I do have a problem." The inspector said, "No you don't." And the owner said, "Yes I do!" The inspector said, "No, sir, you don't." The owner, being unable to contain himself anymore, grabbed the inspector by the arm, pulled him over to the wall, pointed at the cracks, and, with obvious frustration in his voice, the owner says emphatically, "Yes, I do have a problem with my walls!" The inspector finally says, "Sir, you do not have a problem with your walls. The problem is that your house is on a moving foundation. Your house is on unstable ground, and whenever it slides, your walls crack."

A lot of people have cracks on the walls of their lives, and constantly try to cover those cracks with a quick fix. The problem is, if they don't settle upon a sure stable foundation, more cracks are going to keep showing up in their lives.

The stable foundation that eliminates cracks in your life is the foundation of excellence. When people lack excellence, they have cracks of mediocrity and "good enough;" they have cracks of laziness and excuses; they have crack everywhere. What they need is a foundation of excellence.

What is excellence, and how can you achieve it?

DO YOUR VERY BEST

Doing your best means giving your all, going all out, and not cutting corners. Doing your best means working as hard as you possibly can. If you work as hard as you possibly can, you will probably be working harder than others, because many people settle for doing "just enough." But don't be fooled-those who work the hardest often get more opportunities and freedom than those who do not, which usually results in more money and more success. Of course there was a time in America's history when this wasn't true. But today, it is truer than ever before.

Jerry Rice is the greatest wide receiver to ever play in the National Football League. He holds practically every record for his position. During his career, Rice broke so many records because he worked harder than most people in the off-season. When his opponents were traveling, resting, and enjoying the off-season, Jerry Rice worked out two times a day, six days a week. In the morning, he did a torturous five-mile trail-run, only stopping at the steepest section to do a series of ten forty-meter uphill sprints, before he completed the run. As the season approached, he stopped running the hill, and instead ran six one-hundred-yard sprints, six eighty-yarders, six sixty-yarders, six forty-yarders, six twenty-yarders, and sixteen ten-yarders with just two and a half minutes between sets. Then, he did three sets of ten repetitions of twenty different exercises- six days a week! To top it all off, he crawled across the parking lot to his car![4]

Being excellent means doing your very best, and pushing yourself to the edges of your potential.

TAKE RESPONSIBILITY

To take responsibility means to recognize that you have the power to choose how you will respond to whatever comes your way. In between every action and your response to that action is a space- a gap- where you have the power to decide how you are going to respond. After the stimulus, and before

---

[4]

http://outside.away.com/outside/magazine/0898/9808hardway.html

your response to that stimulus, you have the power to make a choice about how you are going to handle or address the situation.

In other words, taking responsibility means that you don't blame anyone else for the results you have received or the situation you are in. Those who take responsibility for their lives refuse to make excuses about why something didn't work. Rather, they are proactive, meaning they don't wait for things to happen to them; they make things happen for them. As a result, they usually get better results than those who are merely reactive.

There is a young man that I have had the privilege of working with, and who seemed to have every disadvantage: His father died when he was a child, his mother is an alcoholic, addicted to drugs, and he was a high school drop-out. Rather than making excuses for the cards that life dealt him, this young man returned to school to get his GED, and he recently enrolled in college. It takes him an hour to get to school on public transportation, and an hour to get home after he leaves the library. About a month after school had been in session, I asked him how he was doing in school. He said that he was doing well, but that he didn't have any books for his classes. He couldn't afford to buy them. I asked him how he had been keeping up with his homework assignments, and he told me that he had been staying in the library until his homework was finished, sometimes leaving campus at nine or ten o'clock at night.

Rather than making an excuse about why he couldn't complete his homework, this young man went to the library every night to use the books in the library. Why? He had taken responsibility for his life. He didn't blame his teachers for giving him homework. He didn't blame his mother for being on drugs. He didn't even blame society for the fact that he couldn't afford books. Instead, he took ownership of his situation, and decided to change it. I was so pleased to discover that because of his hard work, this young man received a full scholarship that pays for all of his college tuition and books.

To be excellent means taking responsibility for your life. It means that you refuse to make excuses about why you are where you are in life, and instead taking matters into your own hands.

DEVELOP A HEALTHY SELF-IMAGE

To be excellent, you also need to see yourself as a person of excellence. Now, I'm not saying that you need to lie to yourself and make up some reasons about why you are God's gift to the world. Rather, I am saying that you need to eliminate any limiting beliefs you have in your head that may be causing you to miss out on great opportunities. Why is this so important? Because how you feel about yourself (your self-esteem) is directly related to how you see yourself (your self-image). How you feel determines what you do. In other words, how you see yourself determines how you feel about yourself, and how you feel about yourself largely determines your actions; your actions, when repeated, result in habits, and habits shape character. Character ultimately determines where you will end up.

Also, how much you like yourself is directly related to how well you relate to others. Only people with high self-images relate well with others on a consistent basis, which usually means you will have a better network of acquaintances and greater potential for opportunities. If you reverse that logic, you see that those without a healthy self-image, people will miss out on great friendships, business partners, and opportunities, which you need to be truly successful.

Jesse Jackson, the civil rights leader, came up with a poem that he often recites to remind people about how important they are. The poem says,

> "I am - Somebody. I may be poor, but I am - Somebody! I may be on welfare, but I am - Somebody! I may be uneducated, but I am - Somebody! I may be young, but I am- somebody. I may be small, but I am- somebody. I may have made mistakes, but I am- somebody. My clothes are different, my face is different, my hair is different, but I am- somebody. I am black, brown, or white,

but I am precious in God's sight. I am-
somebody. I speak a different language,
but I must be respected, protected, never
rejected. I must be, I'm God's child."[5]

In the same way, although you may come from
very humble beginnings, you must always remind
yourself that you are somebody very special. You
may have heard it said, "Just because you live in the
ghetto doesn't mean that the ghetto has to live in
you." The same applies to you. Just because you
live a certain place, it doesn't mean that the
negative, depressing, destructive values of that
place have to live in you. You define your situation;
your situation doesn't define you. You are greater
than your situation. In fact, your worth is not tied to
your circumstances, but rather to the fact that you
are created with infinite worth and purpose.

To be excellent means to improve how you see
yourself. It means rewriting the tape of negative
experiences playing in your head, and instead

---

[5] http://yantouch.wordpress.com/2005/05/24/i-am-somebody/

replacing those negative, limiting, self-defeating images with whole, healthy, and flourishing ones.

MAXIMIZE YOUR USE OF TIME

Ralph Waldo Emerson once said, "This time, like all times, is a very good one, if we know what to do with it." What he was saying is that you need to use your time wisely. It is so easy to think you have all the time in the world, especially if you are young, but the reality is that you only have so much time at your disposal.

Those who maximize the use of their time usually get better results because they have focused their energies on accomplishing one thing as opposed to several things. They have learned to exert themselves on things that will get them closer to achieving their goals. The fact is, those who maximize the use of their time usually enjoy more credibility and influence among their friends and associates, which almost always translates into more success.

I remember hearing Oprah Winfrey describe the time when her personal trainer confronted her. She hired him because she wanted to lose weight, but she had developed a habit of showing up late to her workout sessions with him. At first, her trainer was gracious, and gave her the benefit of the doubt for her lateness. But after Oprah was late a few more times, he confronted her saying, "my time is just as valuable as yours, so don't waste it!" Her trainer recognized that time is very important, and he wanted to make sure that he maximized every moment.

In life, you must learn to maximize your use of time by refusing to procrastinate. Many people don't realize that *busy-ness* is a form of *laziness*. It is easy to stay busy doing something, convincing ourselves that we are maximizing our use of time, when in actuality we are doing something that we shouldn't be doing, in order to avoid doing what we ought to be doing. In other words, *it doesn't matter what you do if what you do is not what you are supposed to do.*

Have you ever needed to complete an assignment, chores, or something else, but in order to avoid doing them, you did something else to stay busy? You rationalized your way out of doing what you needed to do. Rather than busying yourself with things that are not a priority, you have to learn to focus your energies on only those things that can help position you for success.

How do you do that? Every Sunday, I like to sit down at my desk, and write out my plan for the week, and schedule things that must get done that week. I make sure I put my most significant responsibilities on my schedule first, so that I don't bog my schedule down with other things that are less important. If I don't put my most important things in my schedule first, then my schedule will be too full for the goals, objectives, and action steps that would move me closer to my goal.

Furthermore, almost every morning I ask myself, "what do I want most out of life?" Then I ask myself, "what do I want least in life?" Then, I ask, "what must I do today in order to get me closer to what I want most, and what must I do today to keep me from what I want least?" That simple exercise of asking yourself questions can help you focus your time and energy for the day. You may also want to ask, "what five things can I be thankful for today?" That is often a good way to focus your mind, and warm your heart for a day of massive action and total fulfillment.

If you are serious about achieving your dreams, then you will use your time wisely. You won't show up late for important appointments. You won't waste three or four hours watching videos and learning new dance moves (unless you want to be a dancer or something- but even then you should be practicing more than watching others). Your time needs to be spent getting better at what you want to do with your life. Why? Because you want to be the best that you can be, and you ultimately become what you think about most. So make sure you are focusing your mind on your dreams, goals, objectives, and action steps so that you can get closer, and not farther, from having the time of your life.

TAKE EDUCATION SERIOUSLY

There are two kinds of education, the kind that others give to you, and the kind that you give yourself. The first kind is the one you receive at school; the second kind is the one you get by reading books that were not assigned to you at school.

You need both kinds. In life, diplomas, degrees, certificates tell people that you are able to finish something that you started. Pieces of paper tell people that you are disciplined, focused, and serious. They also tell people that you are educated, and that you can think for yourself. Although that is not always true, because I have met many people who have degrees but no common sense. Generally, however, a piece of paper gets your foot in the door.

I talk to many young people who say they "hate" school. They feel as though school is not related to their everyday lives. I first tell them that I understand how they feel, because the truth of the matter is, I used to hate school too. I hated reading, I hated writing, and I hated math. I hated being called on in class by my teachers, because I hated being embarrassed every time I gave the wrong answer. After letting people know that I hated school, I let them know that I had to change the way I viewed school. I had to change the way I viewed books. I had to change the way I viewed math. Ultimately, I had to change the way I viewed myself.

Changing my perception was so important because I thought I wasn't as smart as the other students. They always seemed to have the right answers. They had better clothes than me, they had better things than me, and it even seemed like the teachers liked them more than me (I know for a fact some teachers did like other students more than the liked me). Even though those things were true, I had to ask myself, "If I don't take school seriously, how am I going to end up?" It didn't take me long to realize that I would end up like many people in my family who didn't take school seriously. They were working jobs that they hated, they were living in poor neighborhoods, they were living in tiny apartments, they were always fighting over money, and they always seemed miserable. Many of them were in prison, some were alcoholics, and some were addicted to drugs. I know that none of them planned on ending up that way. I also know that society makes it harder on some people than on others. However, I also made up my mind that I refused to be poor, I refused to be on drugs, I refused to be an alcoholic, I refused to live in poor neighborhoods unwillingly, and I refused to be just like a bunch of people that I had grown up around. People who drank, smoked, played dominoes, cards, and talked trash all day.

I decided that even though it would be hard, I was going to take school seriously. I began seeing books as conversations waiting to be picked up. I began to see math as a game or a puzzle that needed to be figured out. I began to see homework as an opportunity to get better as a person. I began to see school as a way out of poverty, depression, and despair. Once I made that decision, I began treating my teachers better, and began developing better relationships with the adults around me. I knew that not all of them really cared about me or my success, but I also know that there were several who genuinely cared about me, and who wanted me to be my best. I developed relationships with those teachers, and to this day, I thank them for pouring much of their lives into me.

That is the kind of education that others give to you. It's the kind that leads to diplomas, degrees, and certificates.

The second kind of education is the kind that you give to yourself. You may not get a degree for this kind of education, but it certainly makes a bigger impression on you. To give yourself an education means that you don't have a teacher, instructor, professor, parent, or some authority figure holding you accountable for the books you read, and the papers you write. You don't have any quizzes, tests, midterms, or final exams to take. This is the kind of education that requires you to buy books on topics that you are interested in. It is the kind of education that causes you to stay up through the night because you are so enthralled by the things you are learning. It is the kind of education that nobody can take away from you.

When I was in college, most of the things I learned were learned from books that were not assigned to me by my professors. I used to complete my assignments for class, and then go to the library and stay there for hours, reading books about rhetoric, argument, philosophy, English, Spanish, geography, politics, law, and society. I became a student whose thirst for wisdom and knowledge was so insatiable that I would often stay at the library until two or three in the morning, even when school was out of session. I often went to bookstores, and just looked through every section, trying to find something that could help me become a better, more knowledgeable person. To this day, I love books, and I have thousands of them that continue to inspire me, sharpen me, and equip me to make a difference in the world.

Although I have degrees, I recognize that what is more important than the degrees is the knowledge that the degrees symbolize and represent.

Remember this: degrees may get you in the door, but only education and character can keep you there. That's why I tell people to take school seriously. The piece of paper tells people that you are worth taking a chance on. To be sure, some of the smartest people I know never went to school, and didn't graduate from college. As smart as they are, many of them have said to me that they regret not taking school more seriously, because their lack of formal education limited the kinds, and amounts, of opportunities they were given.

The fact is, the more school you attend, the more knowledge and wisdom you get, and the more choices you get. Usually, the more you learn, the better your grades, which means you get more acceptance letters from colleges and universities. The more colleges that accept you, the more options you have to attend the best school. Furthermore, the better the school you attend, the better job offers you will get after you graduate. The better the job offers you get after you graduate mean more money, perks, and privileges for you. Therefore, those who take school seriously usually end up with more freedom of choice, and more money in the bank.

What am I saying? You need to take school seriously by going to class, by paying attention to your teachers, by asking questions, doing your homework before you hang out with friends, and visiting your counselors to get their advice.

Now, I am fully aware that going to school, and getting a safe and secure job is not as safe as it used to be. Now, with the changes in our economy, it is sometimes wiser to get the education you need in order to start your own business. My point is this: whether you want to be given a job or you want to create your own job, you need to take your education seriously.

DRESS FOR SUCCESS

People make their minds up about you within the first three seconds of meeting you. The fact is, how you dress influences what people think about you. Therefore, the better you dress, the better your first impression, which results in better relationships, more opportunities, and often more money.

There is a show on MTV called "From G's to Gents," and it emphasizes the importance of appearance and presentation. Farnsworth Bentley, the shows host, takes guys who have thug-life tendencies and wardrobes, and tries to transform them into men of distinction. Those who do not make the transformation well end up getting kicked off the show. In life, people are judging you based on your appearance, and although you may not be on a television show, you can just as likely get kicked off of a job opportunity because of how you dress.

The fact is your clothes are a reflection of your mind and maturity. If you are hanging with your friends, then dress however you like. But if you want to work for a company, then you need to know that they are evaluating you to see if you would be a good person to represent their company's values, mission, and vision.

Have you seen guys and young girls walking around with their pants sagging? It is always interesting to see them try to run. They can't run very fast because they have to keep pulling up their pants, or use one hand to hold up their pants. They can't focus on their goal without being reminded of their sagging pants. Sagging pants are often symbolic of one who is moving very slowly toward their goal in life, if they even have goals.

How are you supposed to dress for Corporate America? You need to get you some dress slacks and a button down dress shirt. If you can afford it, buy a suit and tie, and a nice black pair of dress shoes. Ladies, please, please, please find clothes that are appropriate for a business environment. I tell you this because nobody told me, and I wore some clothes that were very inappropriate for a corporate environment. Remember, gold teeth are a no-no, and tattoos are not helpful. If you are going to get tattoos, put them on places that won't be a distraction to other people with whom you will interact on your job. Unkempt hair is not cute, and you should avoid hairstyles that can be a distraction. If you have pimples or zits, then get you some Proactive or something to fix your problem (it will help your self-esteem too). Also, your pants need to be around your waist, so get you a size that fits your waist, and a belt to hold them up. Remember, your underwear should never show. That is not sexy!

LEARN HOW TO SPEAK PROPER ENGLISH

Just as clothes tell people about your mind, your vocabulary also influences how people see you. People judge you by the words that come out of your mouth. So those who speak proper English sound more educated and focused than those who do not speak proper English. When you have learned to master the English language, it no longer masters you. When you speak, you should seek to express your ideas in clear and cogent ways. When you do so, you will be more understood, persuasive, and successful. Also, those who speak proper English are more marketable to corporate America, and will usually make more money, have more self-confidence, and enjoy more freedom.

What is important for you to remember is that you need to speak the language of your intended audience. If you are around your family, then you can use slang, and speak in a vernacular that is very casual. If you are around associates or others that you are not friends with, then you can speak in a middle-voice in which there is less slang, and is more grammatically correct. If you are speaking to professors or officials, or dignitaries, then you must learn to use language even more masterfully. What I am trying to say is that you must learn to be multi-lingual, able to speak slang, ebonics, proper English, Spanish, your native language, and anything in between. It all depends on your audience.

One way for you to master your ability to communicate is to listen and learn from those who communicate clearly and properly. Also, you should study basic grammar, and learn new vocabulary words on a regular basis. Once you learn those words, use them in sentences and in your daily conversations. You may want to keep a journal of your thoughts, read a lot of books, and pay attention to how great authors use words.

Also, when you speak, be mindful of how loud you are speaking. The volume of your voice should not be so high that everyone around you can hear everything you have to say, even though you are only talking to one person. When you are in a restaurant, the tables around you ought not hear what you are talking about. The same goes when you are at the movies, or on a cell phone. When you are loud, you are being inconsiderate of other people who are around you, who did not do anything to deserve to hear all of your business.

PICK YOUR FRIENDS WISELY

You are also reflection of the company you keep. I once heard someone say to me, "you are a reflection of your five closest friends." I think that is true. If you have friends who are slackers, smoke weed, have bad tempers, are disrespectful to others in authority, then I would not doubt that you have some of those same characteristics yourself.

Friends are those with whom you have a mutual attraction or respect. You are usually most influenced by those you have something in common with. When someone influences you, you become more and more like him or her, whether you choose to or not. It often just happens unconsciously. That's what conformity is about. It is being shaped and molded by the habits, behaviors, and thoughts of your environment.

When I was younger, many of my friends used to do drugs, drink, steal, curse, fight, waste time, and disrespect women. I was just like them. It wasn't until I started to distance myself from them that I realized how bad those behaviors really were, and how blind I was to my own stupidity.

If you are going be excellent, you have to surround yourself with friends and associates who can sharpen you, and make you better. To find the right people to hang with, you need to evaluate your friends by asking yourself which ones are going in the same direction as you. If there are people in your life who are not serious about growing or being great, then cut them off. I know that sounds harsh, but it is true. I am not saying abandon them as much as I am saying, they can no longer occupy much of your time. If there are people in your life who aren't progressing with you, then you need to reconsider that relationship. In reality, you need to spend more time with those who make you better.

To be sure, I am not saying that you can never be around people who are not as "successful" as you, because the truth of the matter is that you need to be around people who have not enjoyed the same privileges and opportunities as you. Why? So that you can help others, and encourage others to become better people. Having said that, though, you need to careful that you don't get adopt any thoughts, habits, or behaviors that bring you down, and cause you to settle for less than your very best.

Also, you should not have to lower your standards in order to make other people feel comfortable with themselves. If other people have a problem with your success, then let it be their problem, and not yours. It's not your fault that other people are jealous of you, and envy you. It's not your fault that others haven't made the same choices as you. At the same time, though, it is not right for you to look down your nose at someone who hasn't experienced as much joy and success as you. Never try to look too good nor talk too wise. If you are successful, and are enjoying the blessings of God, then you don't need to boast about it.

Also, you should never be the smartest, sharpest, wisest person in the group because you will often end up being the person that gives the most, and whom people rely on the most. If you let that happen, you will probably end up making more deposits in others without ever taking time to make deposits in yourself. You will end up being overdrawn, and without sufficient emotional "funds" to achieve your dreams.

Over the last year, our basement flooded several times. We spent thousands of dollars to fix the problem. Even though the man who originally did the work told us that we would never have any water problems again, he was wrong. After a really bad rain, our basement flooded again.

We ended up calling a more reputable company to come to our home to assess and stop the flooding.

They told us that work done previously was merely a band-aid that didn't stop the leak, but only slowed the leak down. They then told us that we needed the whole basement re-done so that we wouldn't have any more problems.

The new company came in, opened up our basement floor, drilled, dug, and installed drain tiles all the way around the lower level of our home in order to prevent flooding in our basement. We haven't had a problem since they fixed our basement. Why? Because our foundation has been secured with work that was done with excellence.

These days, many people seem to talk a good game, but when it comes down to it, they are just talk. They lack the follow through, the integrity, the excellence that is indicative of quality work. If you have any cracks in your foundation, you need to evaluate your life, and begin to make the necessary improvements so that you can make sure you dreams are standing on solid ground? Go through this chapter again, and ask how well you are doing in all the areas I mentioned.

CHAPTER 4:

THE DISCIPLINE OF EXECUTION

You probably could not tell by looking at me now that I used to play football in high school and college. In fact, throughout high school, I won a few all-state awards in football and in track. Over the years, while playing on several different teams, I have noticed that every team has at least two groups of people on it. There are those who are on the team so they can wear the uniform, attract guys or girls, get into games for free, or some other reason. People in this group stand out because, during practices, they are the ones slacking off, they are usually at the back of the bunch, complain the most, give up the fastest, make a bunch of excuses, and ultimately end up on the bench. People in this group gossip about what is wrong with the team, but don't do anything to make the team better. These people are mediocre at best.

The second group of people, however, is just the opposite. They are the ones who are focused during practice. They push themselves to their limit. They are the ones working during the off-season, running routes, shooting baskets, doing cheers, lifting weights, watching tape, listening to the coaches, studying their opponents, and sharpening their game. People in this second group do not want to settle for merely being on the team; they want to win. As a result, they take action to get better every day.

In life, those who are successful don't just *look* the part, but they make sure they *are* the part. In order to achieve your dreams, you must not only envision your destination, plan your route to get there, and be a person of excellence. You must also do a little bit every day to execute your plan- to bring your dreams closer to your reality. Specifically, what kind of things do you need to do in order to make massive movement toward the achievement of your dreams?

LIGHTEN YOUR LOAD

I used to run track. Before I began my workout, I used to train by tying a tire, and sometimes a parachute, around my waist, and running as fast as I could. The resistance from the tire or parachute made me a much stronger, faster runner. However, they also prevented me from running at my maximum potential. They slowed me down. When the time came for me to compete in various track meets, I not only took off my parachute and tire, I also took off anything that would slow me down. Why, because I wanted to run as fast as I possibly could, and those weights would have slowed me down.

In the same way, you may have some things in your life that you need to take off because they are slowing you down, and preventing you from running at your maximum potential. Nothing is neutral except time. Either something is bringing you closer to realizing your dreams or it is pulling you further away from your dreams. It may not be a bad thing per se, but it is still weighing you down, or holding you back.

You may have some baggage that you need to put down. Perhaps you didn't pick it up on your own, maybe it was something that happened to you. Maybe you were abused as a child- told you were ugly, fat, or at least treated like you were, and it is hindering you, it's holding you back.

What is there in your life that is weighing you down, or holding you back? What is there in your life that needs to be cut off for your very survival? What is there in your life- who is there in your life- that is holding you back? What is there- who is there- in your life that is about to lead you to destruction? What attitude, what mindset needs to be laid aside? What relationship needs to be cut off? What behavior needs to be released? What habits need to be broken? What tendencies need to be eliminated? What proclivities need to be thrown out? What vocabulary words need to be trashed?

To be sure, I am aware that you may have been hurt, and you have not been able to get over it. Perhaps you have been carrying the weight of that pain with you for a long time. The weight is very heavy, but because you have had it for so long, you have gotten used to carrying it. Maybe you have convinced yourself that you deserved it, that you are to blame for it, or something similar to that. I want to tell you that you are not to blame for many of the things that happened to you in your life. I want you to be free- free from that misery, free from that depression, free from those feelings you have been carrying around. To do that, you have to make up your mind that you are so sick and tired of being sick and tired of that burden. You have to decide that you are going to do something to free yourself from it; that you are going to release it once and for all. You have to make up your mind that you are not going to let that burden or weight destroy you, and hold you back any longer. If you need counseling, seek counseling. If you need to forgive someone, then begin working in that direction immediately. You must cut off, release, throw overboard, and destroy anything that is holding you back. If you don't release it, what are you going to miss out on? Take action today to address that burden.

PRESS TOWARD YOUR GOAL

After letting go of any unnecessary weight, you have to take massive action to get closer to your goal. You have to press toward your goal. Pressing involves not merely unloading any unnecessary weight, but it also involves straining forward to attain your dreams. It involves perseverence, it involves heart, and it involves tenacity. It requires that you set your eyes on the goal that is in front of you, refusing to waver until you have reached that goal. The point that I want to make is that your goal must precede your pressing. That means that you must have your eyes on the goal before you begin pressing in that direction.

That might sound like common sense to you, but you would be surprised at how many people are busy but don't have any clear destination or goal in sight. They are just busy pressing without any clear direction. It is important to press toward your goal on a daily basis, or else someone else will have a goal for you to press towards. If you are not careful, you are going to burn out. There are so many things today that are being used to wear you out. There are people pulling you on your job; clubs asking you to do something; people pulling you to do this; other people pulling you to do that.

If you just pay attention to what you hear and see in the media for one day, you will see that music is telling us to do one thing, television another, and internet still another. The tragedy is that we are getting pulled in so many directions that we end up burning ourselves out. We are so busy pressing in all kinds of different directions, that we don't realize that we are not pressing in the direction that matters.

In life, if you are not clear about your goal, then you will be running aimlessly, shadow-boxing a fake target that will wear you out.

So I ask you, in love, what are you pressing towards? You ought not run aimlessly, or like someone boxing the air, without a clear target, or a clear goal. If you don't have the right goal in mind, then you are going to end up at the wrong destination. So, my question to you is, towards what goal are you pressing today? In what direction are you headed? Are you headed toward the goal of being what you were created to be? After you are done reading this chapter, figure out what you are going to do today to move you one step closer to your goal. Take massive action.

GO THROUGH SOMETHING

A man found a cocoon of the emperor moth and took it home to watch it emerge. One day a small opening appeared, and for several hours the moth struggled but couldn't seem to force its body past a certain point.

Deciding something was wrong, the man took scissors and snipped the remaining bit of cocoon. The moth emerged easily, its body large and swollen, the wings small and shriveled. He expected that in a few hours the wings would spread out in their natural beauty, but they did not. Instead of developing into a creature free to fly, the moth spent its life dragging around a swollen body and shriveled wings.

The constricting cocoon and the struggle necessary to pass through the tiny opening are God's way of forcing fluid from the body into the wings. The "merciful" snip was, in reality, cruel. Sometimes the struggle is exactly what you need to prepare you for success.

My point is that you don't get a degree without studying; you don't get a happy marriage without work; you don't get a happy home without sacrifice; you don't get in shape without exercise; you don't get good children without time; you don't teach good lessons without study; your promotion isn't going to come without hard work; your graduation isn't going to come without discipline. You have to go through something to get to your destination!

PACE YOURSELF

The race to your dreams is not going to be easy. The word for race in Greek is where we get our word for "agony." Your race is going to be challenging. Sometimes you are going to cry, want to give up. However, when the going gets tough, remind yourself that the race to success is not a sprint; it is more like a marathon.

In high school, a friend of mine was selected to run the 800-meter race in a track meet against our cross-town rival. The problem was that he had never run the race before that day. The person who was supposed to run had injured himself, and was unable to compete. So my willing and eager friend, positioned in the starting blocks, heard the gun, and burst out of the blocks like he had just stolen something. He sprinted, leaving all the other runners in the dust.

Literally, he was at least 100 meters ahead of everyone else on the track. Once he had run one lap (400 meters), he threw his hands in the air in total victory!

The problem was that he had another lap to go! So we all began screaming at him, urging him to keep running. When it finally hit him that he needed to run another lap, he did his best to make it around the track one more time, but he was too tired to do so. All the other runners flew by him. It took him about four more minutes to make it to the finish line. While he was a fast runner, he failed to pace himself for the race that was at hand.

In your own journey to achieving your dreams, you need to pace yourself. You may want to put this book down today with great enthusiasm and begin "sprinting" toward your goal. You're saying in your head, "I'm going to lose 10 pounds this week; I'm going make one thousand dollars every day. The problem with trying to do too much too soon is that you will soon burn yourself out, and you will end up where you started off. Instead of sprinting, you need to pace yourself. Too many people are lying on the side of the road to their dreams because they started too fast.

You must condition yourself for the long haul, because the difference between successful people and unsuccessful people is the difference of their habits. Good habits are the secret of success. Therefore, form good ones, and become their slave. If you want to lose weight, start off realistically, and walk 3 days a week. After you have developed a good consistency, then try to pick up the length of the exercise, and the intensity. The habit-the consistency- will benefit you more in the long run than a spurt here and there.

TURN THE PAGE

Let's say you have tried something and you fail. What then? What do you do when something you have tried doesn't work? What do you do when the vehicle you just knew would get you to your destination dies on you? The business that you knew was your ticket to financial freedom has failed. The toy you used to love breaks on you. The best friend you believed you would grow up with moves away. The application to your dream school gets rejected. The promotion you were depending on is given to someone else. The dream of a perfect marriage has died because of some tragic discovery. The company you loved has now downsized or restructured you out of a job. The physique that used to be so irresistible has died. The influence you once had has now died because of some mix up. The dependability of those who raised you is now gone, and it's your responsibility to support them. The capacity to give birth has now left you because of life's swift transitions. That which once defined your manhood is no longer attentive. The friends you grew old with have now passed on. What do you do when the vehicle, the thing, the strategy, the action plan, or the person you hoped would take you to your destination has died?

What else can you do, but turn the page? There's no reason to try erasing your mistake, to backspace it, to white it out. That chapter of your life has already been completed, the ink has already dried, and the manuscript has already been sent to publication. So all you can do is turn the page. No need in trying to re-write the chapter, burn the book, or throw it away. It is done. You have to learn from it and turn the page.

Maybe before you picked up this book, you thought your "book" was finished, but the fact is, there is another chapter for your life. It is greater than the last one. But you have to learn to turn the page. You have been re-reading that last chapter, you have been internalizing the fact that you didn't get that job, you didn't get that promotion; you didn't get that guy; you didn't get that home; you didn't get into that school; or, you didn't do well in that subject. You have to turn the page. It's done.

How do you turn the page properly? You first learn from the situation by figuring out how you got into the situation in the first place, and then ask yourself how you can avoid getting into that situation again. You need to learn to see your failures as education. Indeed, you need to learn how to fail forward by learning from your mistakes, getting up again, and trying something new. Don't allow yourself to get paralyzed by fear of failure. Rather, use fear as a means to motivate you to try something new.

Learn to fail early and responsibly. That's what fear stands for: Failing Early And Responsibly. That means rather than missing out on the education that you could get from trying something new, take a risk, and if it doesn't work out, learn from it. That's what it means to fail responsibly. Learn from your mistakes, learn from what didn't work, and try something new. If that doesn't work, learn from it, and try something new.

Many great scientists failed thousands of times before they made a scientific discovery. You have to get comfortable with not getting it right the first time. Failure doesn't mean making a mistake;

rather, failure is not getting up after you have made a mistake. That's massive failure. When you try something, and it doesn't work, turn the page, and write a new chapter in your life.

AWAKEN THE GURKHA WITHIN

To take action, you need to be courageous enough to take risks. In Nepal and India, there is a group of people known as Gurkhas. They are considered to be people who are naturally warlike and aggressive in battle, and possess resilience, physical strength, and courage, among other things.

In 1964, there was a war taking place between Malaysia and Indonesia. And the Malaysian government asked a group of Gurkhas from Nepal if they would be willing to jump from transport airplanes into combat against the Indonesians. However, the Gurkhas had never been trained for that kind of combat. But the Gurkhas agreed to jump from planes under three conditions. "What are they?" asked the military officer. First, they said they would jump from the plane if it flew at a slow speed. Second, the land had to be marshy or reasonably soft and nowhere near rocky mountains because they were inexperienced at jumping from planes. The last thing the Gurkhas requested was that the planes fly only 100 feet from the ground.

The British soldier said that the Gurkhas would be dropped over a jungle, so their landing would be soft. Second, he said that the planes always fly as slowly as possible. Third, however, the British soldier said that it would not be wise for the planes to fly 100 feet from the ground because that would not give the parachutes enough time to open from that height.

The Gurkhas said, "Oh, that's all right then. With parachutes, we'll jump anywhere. Nobody said anything about parachutes before." The Gurkhas were willing to jump from planes without parachutes in order to win the war!

In order to take action, you have to be courageous enough to try something that others would consider to be crazy. You need to be willing to take risks, and put yourself on the line.

"ROLL" YOUR WORKS TO GOD

There is a proverb that says, "Commit your works to the Lord, and your plans will succeed." The word "commit" literally means, "roll." In the Middle East, thousands of years ago, when someone died, and their body was laid to rest in a cave, people in those days would roll a big, heavy stone in front of the cave's entrance, to secure the body. They would "commit" that stone to the cave's entrance.

Sometimes our day-to-day duties seem so heavy, our responsibilities seem overwhelming, sometimes the little things you have to do every day seem so laborious and difficult that you don't have enough time in the day to get things done. You have to do your homework, memorize your playbook, go to that party, buy new clothes, pay your phone bill, exercise, cook, clean, wash, change the diaper, pay the bills, exercise, spend quality time, study, go to class, go to practice, find time to eat, pick the kids up, drop the kids off, pay the mortgage, grade papers, discipline kids, fix a sink, wash a car, an important appointment...your weight just seems too heavy.

I want to encourage you to push our daily "works" to God. To roll our works to God means that you are doing it with God's will in mind. I believe that if we ask anything according to God's will, God will hears us and help us. If the boulders you are rolling are according to His will, He will establish your plans. He will bring them to pass, He will make them successful. If you are rolling your works to God, and your works are according to God's will, your plans will succeed.

There is no shortcut to your dreams. You need to plan your work; and work your plan. You are going to have to work hard every day to make it happen. Every day you wake up, you need to plan your day so that you can move one step closer to achieving an action strategy, an objective, a goal, and yes, your dreams. It will not be easy, but it is possible. The only place where "success" comes before "work" is in the dictionary.

Believe in yourself, take massive action, roll your plans to God, and sooner or later, you will find yourself enjoying the freedom and success you have always dreamed of.

CHAPTER 5:

POWER MENTORING

Most of the world's most successful people had role models who inspired and guided them. A mentor has been there, done that, become a successful person in that industry that you want to enter. They have been down the path, and can help you get there.

It is so important that you find someone who has already achieved the results you want, find out what they are doing, and do the same thing. The fact is, if we plant the same kinds of seeds, we are going get the same kinds of results. It doesn't matter if you are black, white, mexican, asian, poor, rich, or none of the above. What matters is that you excellerate your growth by learning the mentalities and methods of others who are successful at what you want to do.

I often hear people say, "experience is the best teacher." While I believe that experience can be one of your best teachers, I do not believe that it is always the best teacher. Yes, if you want to become masterful at something, you have to keep working at it. For example, if you want to become a great speaker, then you need to find opportunities to speak, or create them. If you want to become a great musician, then you have to constantly practice your instrument. If you want to become a great entrepreneur, then you have to work at running a business. Having said that, however, you need to remember that experience is not always the best teacher. Rather, *other* peoples' experience can be your best teacher.

In order to find a mentor, the first thing you need to do is figure out what type of mentor you need. There are several types of mentors that you may want to consider.

EDUCATIONAL

You want to find you some teachers, administrators, and counselors in your school who can give you the guidance you need to become the person you want to one day become. I know that there are some bad teachers and administrators who do not really care about you, and who only work for a paycheck. I have had plenty of those kinds of teachers. However, I have had the privilege of being mentored by educators who really poured their lives into me.

Erin Gruwell was one of those persons. She inspired me to want more for myself. After I returned to school my sophomore year, I had ambitions to go to college, but I had no idea about what I needed to do to prepare myself for college. I didn't know about the ACT, SAT, requesting college applications, or letters of recommendation. I did not know how to write a personal statement. Fortunately, I had the privilege of meeting a twenty-three year old student-teacher named Erin Gruwell. Erin helped me apply to the University of California at Berkeley. She modeled for me what I needed to do and be in order to go to college.

My mother had given me the confidence, and the passion; Erin Gruwell had given me the guidance. I needed both.

If you are in school, or desire to return to school, you too need to find you an Erin Gruwell who can help give you the guidance and direction you need in order to go the next level in your life.

FINANCIAL

You want to also find someone who can help you acquire and manage your money. If you want to be wealthy, then you should study the methods of people who are wealthy. You need to ask them what they did to become so successful. You need to find out what their habits are, their philosophies and strategies. You need help putting together a budget, and learning how to balance your checkbook. You need someone to help you think about investing in stocks, bonds, and real estate.

A couple of people who inspire me are Donald Trump, Robert Kiyosaki, Napolean Hill, and many other people you probably have never heard of. All of these men are extremely wealthy, and know what it takes for others to get wealthy as well. I study books written by them, and apply many of the lessons they teach. I speak from experience when I say that what they teach actually works.

PHYSICAL

You want to also find someone to help you become more healthy. If you are not in good shape physically, then you are not going to be able to enjoy your success. Find a trainer, a coach, an athlete that you can exercise with. Find out what they eat, and what they don't eat. Find out what kinds of exercise they do, and how often they do them. Find out what their habits are so you can emulate them, and get the same results that they are getting.

RELATIONAL

You want to also find someone who is great at developing relationships. There are some people who can walk into any room, and begin a conversation with anyone, because he or she is a good at starting and building relationships. You want to learn as much as you can about how to open a conversation, how to engage people, how to build trust, and establish comfort. You want to know how to encourage other people, and build them up. You want to learn how to tend to someone who is grieving, and comfort people who are not well.

Also, you want to find someone who has the ability to attract your dream husband or wife. Some people have the ability to attract the most beautiful women, and some women have the ability to hook the hottest guys (not that I would know what a "hot guy" looks like). Rather than being jealous of them, you want to learn what they do to attract women or men. You want to learn how they think, how they dress, how they carry themselves, how they speak, and all the good things that go into a great relationship.

SPIRITUAL

You want to also find you someone who can help you attend to your soul. You need someone who is a spiritual mentor to ask you the hard questions about yourself. You need someone to be able to call you out by pointing out things in your life that need to be addressed. You need someone to ask you about your integrity. My mentors are older pastors to whom I can go for advice, and prayer. Dr. John Woodbridge, Dr. Grant Osborne, Dr. Michael Bullmore, Dr. Greg Scharf, Dr. Perry Downs, and a few others have made me a much better man and servant of God.

FAMILIAL

You also need mentors who ask you questions like, "how are you treating your wife and kids?" "When you are away from home, who keeps you accountable?" There are a few cherished mentors in my life who ask me these hard questions, and challenge me to become a more loving husband and father.

You need older women around you to share their wisdom about life with you, and can help you become a better wife, a better mother, and a better person.

Men like the Rev. Mark Dennis, Rev. K. Edward Copeland, Rev. Dr. Robert Long, Rev. Daniel Robinson often ask me questions that challenge me to become a better family man.

PROFESSIONAL

It is so important for you to find a role model or mentor who is doing what you want to do professionally. If you want to be a lawyer, you need to find a lawyer as your mentor. If you want to be a motivational speaker, you need a mentor to guide you. If you want to be a doctor, then you need to spend time getting advice and guidance from a doctor. Whatever it is you want to do, remember that you are not the first one to do it (most of the time). Therefore, don't make things harder on yourself than they need to be.

The fact is, you do not need to try drugs to learn that they are not good for you. You don't need to go to jail in order to learn that it is somewhere you don't want to end up. You don't need to mismanage your money to learn that bankruptcy hurts. If you want to be successful, then you want to learn from the mistakes of others. Instead of reinventing the wheel, and wasting time, you can learn from others, and find out what they did in order to succeed.

In life, you want to find yourself life coaches or mentors who can bring out the best in you. You want to be influenced by people who are successful in different areas of life. Some people are stronger in, say finance, than they are in relationships. That doesn't make them a bad person; it just makes them better at finance. Get advice from them about finances, and not relationships.

I once read a proverb that says, "If you listen to constructive criticism, you will be at home among the wise."[6] You want to find a mentor, guidance counselor, advisor, or someone who knows something about how to get from where you are to where you want to be.

There may be other people in your life that you could ask for advice right now. Maybe they are friends of your parents, your next-door neighbor, or someone else. Sometimes, the people who can help you are right around the corner from you, and are waiting for someone to ask them for their advice.

Also, I've learned that people like to talk about themselves. An elderly man that I used to visit, Mr. Willie Harris, was one hundred years old when I met him. I used to hang out with him about once a month, and learn about life from him. He had traveled the world, had seen many of the world's great monuments, and he had even ridden his bicycle from Arkansas to Ohio! He was full of stories, and was a storehouse of wisdom. He once

---

[6] Proverbs 15:31

told me, "When you are in the presence of greatness, just shut your mouth and listen, because you never know what you might learn!" As direct as that may seem to you, I appreciated that lesson. I have been around many great people, and always remember to pay close attention to what they are saying. By doing so, I have never left a conversation without learning something new, and helpful, about life and success.

I didn't grow up with many positive role models. Most of the people I looked up to were seasoned criminals, con artists, hustlers, and drug-users. But when I decided to take school seriously, and break the cycle of poverty, and mediocrity in my family, I began to pick up books and learned to love reading. I often went to the library and skimmed books that looked interesting, and I learned very quickly that *books are conversations waiting to be picked up.*

I have always wished that I could have met and served with the Rev. Dr. Martin Luther King, Jr., and other great people in history. I sometimes imagined what it would be like to soak up their wisdom like a sponge. Since I didn't have a time machine, I did the next best thing: I read many of the books that they had written. I used to sit down for hours and just drink from the rich fountains of their wisdom, and learn about their values, strategies, missions, and visions.

To this day, if you want to find me in my leisure time, you will probably find me in a bookstore, library, in a park, or on a bench with a book and a journal.

I have learned that you success leaves clues, and you thus need to study those who have done what you want to do. You can save yourself years of experience, and mistakes, by taking the time to read about the experiences and mistakes of others. If you want to be a great singer or rapper, then you need to study the lyrics, beats, riffs, runs, and techniques of great singers and rappers; if you want to be great, you have to study, and learn from those great people who have gone before you.

Who has done, or is doing, what you want to do with your life? Name three or four people who are doing what you want to do, and write their names down in the margins of this book right now. Have they written any books that you can buy or check out at the library? Have they made any DVDs or CDs that you can study? Have they done any interviews that you can watch, and learn from? Take time to research what they have done, and make time to study them. Their hard-earned wisdom could save you a lot of time, hurt, money, and energy.

If you want to take matters into your own hands, follow the guidelines that have been laid out in these pages:

D stands for Dream, and it is a reminder that you need to know where you are going before you can begin moving in that direction. Your dream is your compass and your DNA. It drives you, motivates you, and gives you purpose, hope, and direction.

R stands for Roadmap. Once you have you dream, you need to have a roadmap to get you from where you are to where you are going. I have laid out a simple plan for you to begin writing down your own map toward your journey.

E stands for Excellence. To get from where you are to where you want to end up, you are going to need to practice excellence in all that you do.

A is for Action, because your dreams will never get out of your head and into your reality until you actually take action. You need to do something everyday to reduce the distance between your present state and your dream.

M is for Mentors. You can save yourself plenty of time, energy, and resources if you learn from others who have done what you want to do. You can learn from their trials and triumphs, and apply some of their wisdom to your own situation.

That spells out DREAM. If you will do these things, the things you used to call dreams will become a part of your daily reality.

I hope you have taken the words on these pages seriously, and figured out what you really want in life, and have put that plan down on paper. I also hope that you commit to practicing the art of excellence, take massive action, and find mentors to guide you.

If you will use what you already have, then you will have TAKEN MATTERS INTO YOUR OWN HANDS. You won't have to live your life with regrets, wondering, "what if I tried this, or what if I did that." No, by taking matters into your own hands, you took a chance on yourself.

There is a scripture in the Bible where God asks Moses, "What is that in your hand?" When God asked the question to Moses, God was not trying to get information. God knew exactly what was in Moses' hand. It was a staff. The reason God asked the question was to let Moses know what he had in his hand. To Moses, it was probably just a little stick, but to God, it was so much more.

I ask you today, what's that in your hand? What dream, what gift, what skill, what talent? I don't ask for information; I ask to let you know that you already possess more than you realize. You possess more creativity, more ability, more power, and more greatness than you realize. Take what's in your hand, use it with all your might, and it will take you to your destiny. That is the "road less traveled." That is taking matters into your own hands.

AFTERWORD:

THE PURSUIT OF HAPPINESS

An old African sage, wise and influential, lived on the side of a mountain near a lake. It was common practice for the people of the village to seek his advice. The old man spent many hours sitting in front of his small hut, where he rocked in a crude rocking chair made of branches and twigs. Hour after hour, he sat and rocked as he thought.

One day he noticed a young African warrior walking on the path toward his hut. The young man walked up the hill and stood erect before the sage. "What can I do for you?" the old man said.

The warrior replied, "I was told by those in the village that you are very wise. They said that you could give me the secret of happiness and the good life."

The old man listened, then gazed at the ground for several moments. He rose to his feet, took the boy by the hand, and led him down the path back toward the lake. Not a word was spoken. The young warrior was obviously bewildered, but the sage kept walking. Soon they approached the lake, but did not stop. Out into the water, the old man led the boy. The farther they walked, the higher the water advanced. The water rose from the boy's knees to his waist, then to his chin, but the old man said nothing and kept moving deeper and deeper. Finally the lad was completely submerged. At this point the wise man stopped for a moment, turned the boy around, and led him out of the lake and up the path back to the hut. Still not a word was spoken. The old man sat again in his creaky chair and rocked to and fro.

After several thought-provoking minutes, he looked into the boy's questioning eyes and asked, "young man, when you were in the lake, underwater, what was it you desired most?"

Openly excited, the boy replied, "Why, you old fool, I wanted to breath!"

Then the sage spoke these words: "My son, when you want happiness in life as badly as you wanted to breathe, you will have found the secret."[7]

Like that young warrior, we all are in search for happiness. I have tried to lay out in this book lessons that I've learned that will lead to your success. What I have not done is lay out how to be happy. It is true, if you are successful, and have earned a lot of money, and purchased several nice things, that you could be content with your place in life.

While that may be true, I have come to learn that there is a big difference between success and happiness.

People want to be happy. Most people do things, or avoid things, in order to be in a state of happiness. The fact is, we want to be successful, because we really want happiness, joy, and fulfillment. I suspect that Will Smith's movie, the

---

[7] Dennis Kimbro, Think and Grow Rich, Fawcett Publishing, 1992.

"Pursuit of Happyness," has done so well because deep down inside, all of us are, or once were, in pursuit of happiness.

Of all of the things I want you to be, my hope is that you will be happy.

Because I respect you, and care so much about you, I could not end this book without sharing with you the most important part of my life that gives me happiness.

I was born into a beautiful, yet very broken family. My father was in prison for most of my life, my Latina mother was disowned by her father for giving birth to me, an African-American child, and, my step-father was, at times, a belligerent alcoholic who at times physically abused my mother whenever he went on one of his binges.

For much of my childhood, we moved from place to place, trying to find some kind of stability. But by the time I was sixteen, I had already lived in twenty-six different places, not including the shelters, cars, and motels we slept in. There were many nights when the only meal we had was a piece of bread and a cup of soup; and, the only blanket I had was my mother's jacket, as I slept on the cold concrete floors of homeless shelters.

Around that time, I began experimenting with drugs, drinking alcohol, and breaking the law. I started burglarizing homes, stealing cars, and robbing people. I also stopped caring about school. For much of my youth, I missed sixty to ninety days of school per year.

My first semester in high school, I earned a 0.6 G.P.A. In fact, my English grammar was so poor that I was classified as an ESL student (English as a Second Language) (I think it was because I used to use really "big" words in the wrong way on my tests).

The next semester of my freshman year, my best friend, Alexander "Alex" Giraldo, was on his way to my house when he was brutally murdered.

When I went to see his remains, I remember seeing my best friend in a casket, where I could see the marks from the murder upon his lifeless form. I will never forget the sobs coming from his little sister who was curled up on the floor near the casket.

Seeing Alex in that casket, in that way caused something inside me to die with him.

Shortly after Alex's death, I dropped out of high school, and began engaging in more behavior that would have ended in my incarceration or death.

My soul was crying out with the poet, Paul Lawrence Dunbar, when he said:

A crust of break, a corner to sleep in,
A minute to smile, an hour to weep in;
A pint of joy to a peck of trouble,
And never a laugh, but the moans come double-
And that is life!

My heart was also weeping with the philosopher Schopenhauer who declared that "life is an endless pain with a painful end."

It was in that pit of despair, in that quagmire of misery, that I reached ground zero. I was broken, depressed, and empty. Something had to change.

Isn't it amazing how God sends people into your life at just the right time to give you exactly what you need? That's what happened to me.

I was sitting alone on a park bench in Long Beach, California when a man named Martin Stokes approached me, and began to tell me his story. He said he was once addicted to cocaine, and that it caused him to lose everything- his job, his house, his wife, and his family.

Martin said he was sleeping behind a dumpster when a local pastor found him, took him in, and helped him to turn his life around.

He helped me see that anyone can change with the right help.

Martin began to share the gospel of Jesus Christ with me- that God loves me more than I could ever understand, and that Jesus Christ died on a cross so that I could receive life.

That message helped me see beyond my present circumstances, and gave me a glimpse of a brighter future for myself. Martin helped me see that I could break the cycle of pain and poverty in my family. He helped me see that I could create a better life for myself and my family. He helped me see that I could become the kind of father that I never had. He helped me see that I could use my pain to empower others, and give people hope. And, he helped me see that I needed to return to school to make all of those things happen.

That conversation, on that park bench, about the gospel of Jesus Christ, and my decision to invite Christ into my life, gave me a sense of peace and contentment that I had never, ever experienced.

I felt a presence in me that was not there before.

I know that may sound crazy, and spooky, or whatever- trust me, that's what I would normally think if someone told me something like that. But please hear me when I say that my heart was changed. I was freed to love people in a way that I never felt before. Much of the anger that crippled me was gone. I was finally happy.

After that experience, I returned to school, made it to the honor roll, was placed in Erin Gruwell's class, graduated from high school, from college, from graduate school, and enjoy the many blessings that have come my way since that experience.

I share that with you to impress upon you that the happiness I now enjoy has very little to do with the things that I own, the places I have traveled, or the things I have done. Don't get me wrong. I enjoy the nice things, the great trips, and the wonderful experiences. But my happiness goes back to the person I met on that park bench years ago- Jesus Christ.

Now, please believe me when I say that I am not here to force my faith on you in any way. Actually, my Christian faith teaches me that only those who are drawn to Christ by the Spirit of God can actually come to know Christ like I did on that park bench.

So, I'm really here to ask you if you are on a "bench" in your own life, and if you are open to hear more about Jesus Christ.

I have spent the last eight years of my life examining the archeology, the history, the earliest ancient manuscripts of the Bible; I have studied the non-Christian historians who verify that Christ was a real person who was crucified; I have critically examined the testimonies of people who witnessed Jesus' life, death, and resurrection; I have become a student of Greek and Hebrew (most of the Bible was originally written in those languages); I have taken a look at how much my own life, and the life of many others, has been changed by encountering Jesus Christ; and, I can say with total confidence that Jesus was who He said He was.

Because of the reliability of, and my belief in, what I have researched and experienced, I want to humbly invite you to take an objective look at who Jesus Christ was and is. I wouldn't ask if I didn't care. I do care, so I must ask. If you are interested in finding out more, then check out Timothy Keller's The Reason for God, Anchor for the Soul by Ray Pritchard, J. P. Moreland's Scaling the Secular City, or A.W. Tozer's the Pursuit of God. Or, you could always pick up a Bible and read

Matthew, Mark, Luke, or John. Those books have really touched me in special ways.

Whether or not you honor my request, I have no doubt you will go far if you apply the things I've written about in this book. I haven't done so bad myself. For that I am very grateful.

There's an old song that I love so much. It says,

If I can help somebody as I pass along,
If I can cheer somebody with a word or song,
If I can show somebody he is trav'ling wrong,
Then my living shall not be in vain.[8]

These words are precious to me because they remind me that true success and significance will not be measured by material things, but, in the final analysis, success will be measured by how much we have given our lives in service to others.

In this book, I have tried to help you on your journey to significance and success; I have tried to point out things that may be blocking you from

---

[8] "If I Can Help Somebody," A. Bazel Androzzo, © 1945, Alma B. Androzzo

reaching your dreams; and, I have tried to cheer you with words that are life-giving and transformational. If I have done even one of these things for you, then my living has not been in vain.

About the Author

Manuel Scott's story is told in the Hollywood movie, Freedom Writers, starring two-time Academy Award® winner Hillary Swank and Grey's Anatomy's Patrick Dempsey.

Manuel is the founder of Glimpse, a consulting firm, committed to equipping schools, civic organizations, and churches to shake off mediocrity and live up to their greatness. Glimpse accomplishes its goals by training teachers, students, volunteers, and leaders through keynotes, workshops, special presentations, seminars, counseling sessions, books, CDs, and DVDs.

Manuel holds a B.A. from the University of California at Berkeley, and Master of Divinity from Trinity International University. He serves as an Assistant Pastor of the Historic Second Baptist Church of Evanston, IL.

Manuel's customized presentation will teach, inspire, and channel your audience to new levels of achievement.

To find out more about Manuel Scott's activities contact:

Glimpse LLC

P. O. Box #6023

N. Buffalo Grove Road

Buffalo Grove, IL 60089

Phone/Fax: (847) 520-8114

Or visit Manuel's website at

www.manuelvscott.com

info@manuelvscott.com